wet games

a fun approach to teaching swimming and water safety

Peter Meaney
Sarie Culka

illustrated by Georges McKail

First published in 1992 by
Robert Andersen & Associates Pty Ltd
433 Wellington St
Clifton Hill, Victoria
Australia 3068

Reprinted 1994, 1996, 1999, 2001, 2003

National Library of Australia
Cataloguing-in-publication data:

Meaney, Peter H.
    Wet games.

    ISBN 0 949133 28 0.

    1. Swimming for children. 2. Aquatic sports – Safety measures. I.
Culka, Sarie. II. Title.

797.21

Typeset by Bookset
Printed by Openbook Print 0943-03

CONTENTS

FOREWORD

After swimming competitively for the past nine years, I can't imagine life without swimming, especially in Australia. I, too, like many young Australians, went to the local pool or beach with friends during hot school holidays.

There seem to be so many accidents involving water which could be easily avoided by being comfortable in the water and learning water safety skills. The best way to teach swimming is to make it fun, and what better way to have fun than to play games? The children tend to forget that they're in water; they concentrate more on the games and how much fun they're having, and before you know it (and before your children know it, too!) they'll be swimming confidently whilst having a great time.

Wet Games will show you all you need to know about teaching swimming and water safety. It is set out in an easy descriptive manner, which will be easily understood by all.

Good luck!
Yours in swimming,

Nicole Livingstone-Stevenson

INTRODUCTION

Children learn best when they are entertained greatly while being educated gently.

Commodore Longfellow

This simple maxim should be the guiding principle by which those who read this book consider the teaching of swimming. Beginners and advanced swimmers often have preconceived ideas about what is involved in lessons. Usually they envisage the teaching of swimming as restricted to having students swim laps in a number of lanes with or without the use of kickboards — and all too often they are right! Yet any lay person will tell you that learning should be fun and enjoyable, and the learning of swimming is no different from that of any other subject. Through playing games, even the most advanced scientific principles can be taught.

Many of the games and activities in this book have been included to provide participants with new and exciting challenges. However, physical challenges are often accompanied by 'risk taking', and *it is therefore imperative that teachers conduct these activities with* **safety** *being their catchword.* Safety is the **most** important factor in a swimming program and **must never** be deliberately overlooked in the line of 'thrill seeking'. Water must be respected, no matter of what depth or in what location. Participants of all ages and at all levels must be supervised constantly. The activity 'Tied Up' is 'potentially' a risky game that has been included to give participants the opportunity to experience and deal with the problem of becoming entangled under water; for example, in reeds, kelp, fishing lines, rigging from a boat or parachute webbing from parasailing. However, as described in the text, the rope is never knotted and the partner is always in the water first. Should the swimmer get into any difficulty, he or she is merely held against the wall by the free partner — no swimming rescue is necessary.

We have used all games and activities extensively with both children and adults of all ages and at all levels. We have used them with great success on courses for Austswim and the Australian Council for Health, Physical Education and Recreation, in national and international courses, and in primary and secondary schools' swimming programs.

I would like to include words from Dr Bill Belanger, professor at the University of Ottawa, Canada. Bill is an international aquatic educator and recently visited Australia to conduct aquatic seminars.

The immediate concern is that some people may learn to swim very well without learning the related knowledge and skills that are necessary in coping with aquatic emergencies. It is incumbent on every swimming instructor, regardless of their orientation or affiliation, to teach novices the basic safety knowledge, skills and attitudes that will allow them to be safe with the new found swimming skills. Teaching a child to swim leads a child to seek greater challenges and risk in water. Instructors must ensure that children are prepared to cope with these increased risks.

Water safety is not common sense. Common sense is learned from common experience and common experience is dry experience. To be water safe, a wet experience is necessary. It is important to teach the basic water safety rules, but it is more important to develop a wide variety of skills for coping with potential hazards.

People who are involved in somersaulting from a rope, splashing head first from a slide or getting dunked from a rubber mat have experienced a wide range of water safety skills which will give them an advantage if they are surprised in an aquatic emergency.

The purpose of this book, then, is to provide swimming teachers with a number of games and ideas to promote the fun element in learning water skills and safety. The rationale of each game is given, and although the number of participants and basic organisation have been suggested, teachers may adapt or vary these as conditions dictate. Obviously, there is still a place for stroke development within the framework of a lesson, but the book should provide ideas to *enhance* the teaching of swimming and water safety. The games may be used as introductory activities, as main parts of lessons or as concluding activities.

Children and adults love playing in water. As a teacher, encourage this element of play as an integral part of your teaching strategy.

PETER MEANEY

KEY TO SYMBOLS

Difficulty		*Water level*
advanced	✓	deep
intermediate	✓	waist deep
beginner	✓	knee deep

The following abbreviations are used in the text:

EAR   Expired air resuscitation
PFD   Personal flotation device
PID   Person in difficulty

ALPHABET
CARDS

Rationale   To encourage entry and exit skills, and quick response.

Level   Beginner/intermediate/advanced.

Equipment   Large, plastic alphabet cards, one set for each team; list of suitable words.

Depth of water   Shallow to deep, according to standard of players.

Number of participants   Small groups to whole class.

Organisation   Teams lined up along edge, with cards shared between players.

Description   The teacher calls a word (for example, 'swim' or 'race') and the players holding the required letters race across the pool, climb out and form up in order to spell the word. The first team in position wins. The methods of entry, exit and movement through the water may be varied to suit the standard of the players and to add variety to the game.

BALL, HOOP AND BLOCK

Rationale   To encourage submersion for beginners and surface dives for advanced swimmers.

Level   Beginner/intermediate/advanced.

Equipment   One large ball, one weighted hoop for each team, one block for each player.

Depth of water   Shallow to deep, according to standard of players.

Number of participants   Small groups to whole class.

Organisation   Teams of six or eight, across the pool.

Description   Players line up in teams on the edge of the pool, with number 1 holding the ball. On the word 'Go', number 1 enters the water using an entry appropriate to the depth (or an entry designated by the teacher), runs or swims with the ball to the hoop, submerges, passes through the hoop, then turns and throws the ball to number 2. This player repeats the sequence while number 1 turns, swims to the blocks, submerges, retrieves one block, continues to the other side of the pool and climbs out. Player number 6 completes the sequence by carrying the ball and the block to the finish. The first team to finish wins.

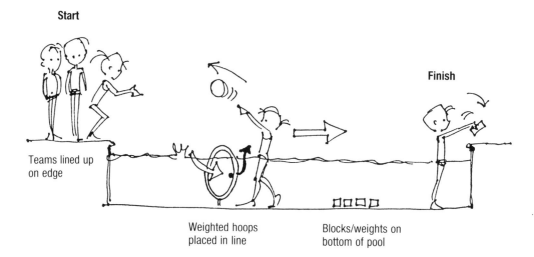

Start

Finish

Teams lined up on edge

Weighted hoops placed in line

Blocks/weights on bottom of pool

2

BALL-JUGGLING TORPEDO

Rationale To develop a strong flutter kick.

Level Advanced.

Equipment 15 centimetre ball or kickboard.

Depth of water Waist-deep.

Number of participants Small groups to whole class.

Organisation Individual players, in relays or other team activities.

Description The individual player lies on his or her back and performs a flutter kick across the pool, meanwhile passing the ball or kickboard from hand to hand with arms fully extended above the body.

Variation Instead of using a ball or a kickboard, home-made water scoops can be constructed from recycled orange-juice containers and the swimmer can pour the water from one container to another.

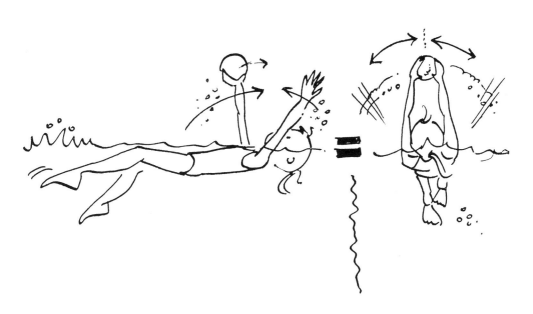

BEACHED WHALES

Rationale   To develop and practise the ability to dive while wearing a personal flotation device (PFD).

Level   Intermediate/advanced.

Equipment   Recognised PFDs, 100 flat (1.25 cm) rubber discs (7.5 cm in diameter), plastic bucket.

Depth of water   Chest-deep.

Number of participants   Up to whole class.

Organisation   In groups of four or five, one group at a time.

Description   The discs are put into the pool and allowed to sink. The teacher — or a member of another group — holds the bucket. Wearing the PFDs, players attempt to retrieve and put into the plastic bucket as many discs as possible in 60 seconds. The winning team will be the one who retrieved the most discs.

BLACKOUT

Rationale   To teach the survival techniques used when unable to see.

Level   Intermediate/advanced.

Equipment   One pair of blackout swim goggles for each player, PFDs or buoyancy aids (optional).

Depth of water   Shoulder-deep to deep.

Number of participants   Small groups to whole class.

Organisation   In pairs (buddy system). If playing in deep water, it is desirable to use the PFDs or buoyancy aids.

Description   Players are paired before putting on the goggles, so that each knows the name of his or her partner. They are then separated and disorientated as much as possible (for example, turned around three times), while the teacher moves so that his or her voice comes from a different direction. Partners first try to find each other by calling and listening, while moving through the water in such a way as to avoid injury to themselves or others; when they meet, they must remain silent and listen for the next instruction. This may be to follow directions given by the teacher or teachers; for instance, to swim towards or away from the sound of a voice, to swim towards the sound of splashing or to listen for a mechanical sound and swim towards it.

   A good activity is to ask the players to form one big circle, with partners keeping in contact, and then to find out how many are in the circle. (This requires that one player take the role of leader.) If the group is small and players know the number, the teacher can quietly extract one from the circle.

BOOGIE-WOOGIE

Rationale   To develop the skill of row rescues.

Level   Intermediate/advanced.

Equipment   One boogie board or small surf mat for each team.

Depth of water   Deep.

Number of participants   Small groups to whole class.

Organisation   Teams of six or eight.

Description   Each team's number 1 player starts on the opposite side of the pool from the rest. On the command 'Go', number 1 dives in on the board, paddles to number 2 and gets off the board. Both players then hold the board, kick back to the starting point and climb out. Number 2 repeats the sequence with number 3, and so on until all players are at the starting point.

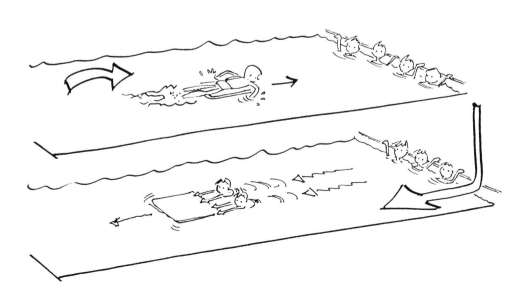

BUCKET TO BUCKET

Rationale   To encourage surface diving and swimming while carrying an object.

Level   Intermediate/advanced.

Equipment   Two weighted buckets and a rubber brick for each team.

Depth of water   Deep.

Number of participants   Small groups to whole class.

Organisation   Each team of four to six in shuttle relay formation, working the length of the pool.

Description   Buckets are approximately 5 metres apart on the bottom of the pool, with the brick in the one nearer the first player. On the word 'Go', the first player dives into the water, swims to the first bucket, surface dives, collects the brick, swims underwater to put it in the second bucket, surfaces again and swims to the end of the pool. Each player repeats this sequence until all have had a turn.

   Note: If necessary, swimmers may surface between the buckets.

BUILDING BRICKS

Rationale   To practise and strengthen the ability to tread water.

Level   Advanced.

Equipment   For each group, one rubber diving brick (about 2 kg).

Depth of water   Deep.

Number of participants   Up to whole class.

Organisation   In groups of four or five.

Description   Each group gets into the water, forms a circle and treads water. The aim is for each player in turn to hold the brick with both hands, keeping the wrists just above the surface, while continuing to tread water. On the word 'Go', the first member of each group attempts to do this for 2 minutes before passing the brick to the next person; 2 points are given to every swimmer who does this, so if there are four swimmers in each team a maximum of 8 points can be obtained. A swimmer who can last only for one minute and a half will score 1½ points, and so on. The winning team will be the one with most points.

CHICKEN WING

Rationale   To develop shoulder flexibility and a good elbow action for the freestyle arm movement.

Level   Intermediate.

Equipment   None.

Depth of water   Waist-deep.

Number of participants   Up to whole class.

Organisation   Individual players.

Description   The swimmers hook their thumbs under their armpits. On the word 'Go', they perform flutter kicks across the pool while rotating their arms, using them as paddles. The thumbs stay locked in the armpits and the water is pulled by the inside of the elbow joints (medial side).

Note that swimmers should breathe by rolling completely onto one side.

Variation   This can be performed as a relay race.

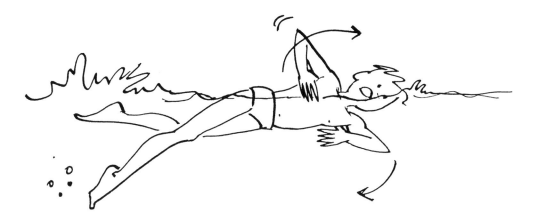

CIRCLE TAG

Rationale   To develop confidence in moving through water.

Level   Beginner.

Equipment   None.

Depth of water   Knee-deep to waist-deep.

Number of participants   Groups of even numbers, from six to whole class.

Organisation   In pairs, numbered 1 and 2 in each pair.

Description   Number 1s join hands and form a circle; number 2s stand outside the circle with their hands on their partners' shoulders. On the word 'Go', everyone skips to the right. When the teacher calls 'One place change', the number 2s leave their partners and each moves to touch the shoulders of the person to the right. The number 1s continue to hold hands and skip around. To make it a lot harder, the teacher can call 'Two places change'.

Variation   When the teacher has called two or three times, the call can be 'stop'. At that point the number 2s swim around the circle (still to the right) until they reach their original partners. They then swim or crawl through the partners' legs and take up the front position.

CITY BRIDGES

Rationale   To develop confidence in water through active movements.

Level   Beginner.

Equipment   None.

Depth of water   Knee-deep to waist-deep.

Number of participants   Up to whole class.

Organisation   Small groups or teams of about six, well spaced.

Description   Two members of each group join hands and form an arch. The remainder of the group stand one behind the other, each holding onto the waist of the person in front and ready to pass under the arch. On the word 'Go' each group, as a 'train', passes first under its own arch and then under every other arch. The first team to pass under all the arches and back through its own will be the winner.

Variation   The teacher may instruct the arches to be lowered, so that towards the end of the game the players must duck under the water to pass below them.

COMMANDO

Rationale   To develop the skill of searching below the surface in murky water.

Level   Intermediate.

Equipment   Blackout goggles, one clear-perspex object for each team.

Depth of water   Chest-deep to deep.

Number of participants   Small groups to whole class.

Organisation   Groups of four to six, each in small area.

Description   The commando unit has parachuted into enemy territory at night. All have landed safely, but the pack of equipment and rations has landed in a small dam. The group must develop a safe method to retrieve it.

All movement will be quiet and efficient: the enemy must not be alerted. Players must demonstrate a safe entry, a method of finding the edge again and a method of judging direction (usually from the voice of one member of the team). Not all team members have to be searching at the same time.

CURLY KELP

Rationale   To develop the technique of swimming through weed or kelp.

Level   Intermediate.

Equipment   Strips of plastic garbage bags attached to weighted hoops (one for each team), clear-plastic bottles filled with water (one for each player).

Depth of water   Deep.

Number of participants   Small groups to whole class.

Organisation   Teams of four.

Description   On the word 'Go', the first team member dives into the water, swims to the weeds, dives and searches for a bottle, retrieves it and swims back to the starting point. Number 2 then has a turn, and so on until all bottles are retrieved.

CURRENT
AFFAIRS

Rationale To encourage the use of only legs for propulsion.

Level Intermediate/advanced.

Equipment One piece of newspaper for each team.

Depth of water Deep.

Number of participants Small groups to whole class.

Organisation Teams of four or six in shuttle relay formation.

Description Each number 1 player holds the team's newspaper. On the word 'Go', number 1 enters the water with the newspaper, swims to number 2 and passes the paper to that player, who swims with it to number 3 and so on. The object of the game is to keep the paper from getting wet. The first team to finish with dry paper is the winner.

DISCO

Rationale   To encourage submersion and the ability to open the eyes underwater.

Level   Beginner.

Equipment   One weighted bucket, with flutter discs numbered 1 to 6, for each team.

Depth of water   Shallow.

Number of participants   Small groups to whole class.

Organisation   Teams of six.

Description   Teams line up in crocodile file on one side of the pool. Buckets are placed on the bottom of the pool, halfway across, with discs inside. The players in each team are numbered 1 to 6. On the word 'Go', number 1 enters the water, wades as fast as possible to the bucket, submerges, finds the number 1 disc, carries it to the other side of the pool and climbs out. Number 2 then repeats the sequence, collecting number 2 disc, and so on until all six players have a disc. They then replace the discs, in order, in the bucket. The first team to complete the activity is the winner.

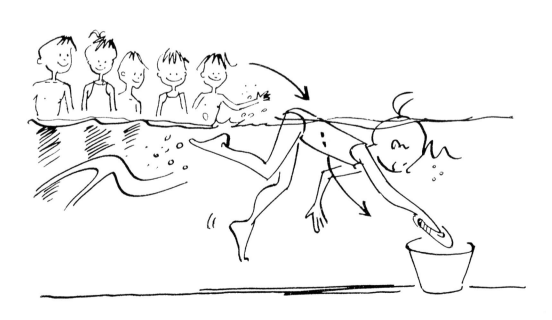

DIVE AND CHASE

Rationale   To encourage the techniques involved in a racing dive.

Level   Intermediate/advanced.

Equipment   None.

Depth of water   Chest-deep.

Number of participants   Small groups to whole class.

Organisation   Pairs working across the pool.

Description   One of each pair is in the water at the side of the pool, ready to swim across; the other stands above, on the side, facing away from the water. The teacher signals those in the water to begin swimming, and when they are a reasonable distance away from the wall gives the command, 'Go'. Those out of the water turn, dive in and give chase to their partners, attempting to 'tag' them before they reach the other side of the pool. The process is then repeated by each pair, but with the roles reversed.

DIVING CLOWNS

Rationale   To practise treading water and feet-first diving.

Level   Advanced.

Equipment   Water-polo balls or equivalent, wooden hoops.

Depth of water   Deep.

Number of participants   Small groups to whole class.

Organisation   Groups or teams of four to six.

Description   Group members tread water, one beside the other, facing a fixed hoop floating on the surface 2 metres away. On the word 'Go', the first person swims with the ball to the hoop, dives, and surfaces inside the hoop. From here he or she throws the ball to the next in line, who throws it back and does a feet-first dive to the bottom of the pool and back to the surface. Meanwhile, the player at the hoop throws the ball to the next person, who dives in turn. When the last in line gets the ball, he or she swims with it to the front of the line and then on to the hoop, while the previous 'hoop person' swims back to the front of the line. When everybody has had a turn in the hoop, the game concludes.

DRAGON BOAT

Rationale   To encourage co-operation and the techniques of arm actions and leg strokes.

Level   Intermediate/advanced.

Equipment   None.

Depth of water   Chest-deep to deep.

Number of participants   Teams of eight.

Organisation   Teams working over at least 25 metres.

Description   Players line up one behind the other at the starting point. On a given signal they link up in the designated grip, which may be either with legs around the waist of the player behind or with hands resting on the shoulders of the player in front. If the leg grip is used, the arms will be used for propulsion in freestyle, breaststroke, backstroke or butterfly actions; for backstroke, all swimmers will begin on the back. If the hand grip is used, propulsion will be by flutter kick or whip kick. On the command 'Go', the 'boat' races to the finish line.

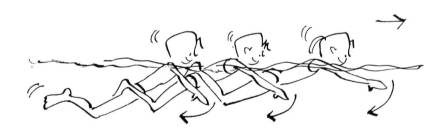

THE DREDGER

Rationale   To increase the strength of the freestyle kick.

Level   Advanced.

Equipment   Kickboard for each player.

Depth of water   Waist-deep to deep.

Number of participants   Small groups to whole class.

Organisation   Individual players or teams.

Description   Each person uses a flutter kick to cross the pool holding the kickboard outstretched in front, vertical, and at least 30 centimetres below the surface. This may be played as a relay in which the number 1 of each team passes the kickboard on to number 2, and so on.

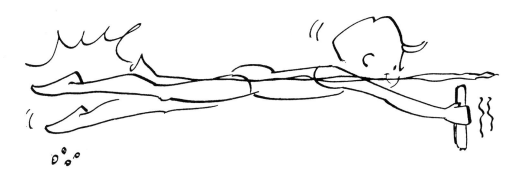

DUCK-DIVE RELAY

Rationale   To develop the techniques used in surface diving.

Level   Intermediate.

Equipment   One diving brick and one target area for each team.

Depth of water   Waist-deep to deep.

Number of participants   Small groups.

Organisation   Teams of four to six.

Description   Teams stand in crocodile line against one side of the pool, facing the other side. Before starting, the brick for each team is placed in the target area. On the word 'Go', team member 1 swims out, duck-dives to retrieve the brick and carries it to the starting line. Number 2 then carries it back to the target area, duck-dives to replace it and swims back to the team. This continues until each member of the team has had a turn.

Variation   Each person swims to the target area, duck-dives to retrieve the brick, treads water for 10 seconds and duck-dives to replace it.

EGGHEAD

Rationale   To improve leg action when treading water and to further strengthen the eggbeater kick.

Level   Advanced.

Equipment   None.

Depth of water   Deep.

Number of participants   Small groups to whole class.

Organisation   In pairs.

Description   Partners face each other, treading water, each with a hand on the top of the other's head. On the command 'Go', each tries to push the other under the water.

ESCAPE FROM ALCATRAZ

Rationale   To encourage conservation of energy and to develop some survival techniques.

Level   Beginner/intermediate/advanced.

Equipment   Markers on the edge of the pool, optional use of clothing, kickboards or underwater 'hazards'.

Depth of water   Waist-deep to deep.

Number of participants   Small groups to whole class.

Organisation   Either one or two swimmers at a time, or groups of seven or eight.

Description   The players start at one end of the pool. They enter the water, swim a designated distance, submerge, swim underwater a designated distance, surface, swim to the end and climb out. During this sequence they must take care to make no sound, no splash, no ripple on the surface; otherwise, they are 'shot'. They are also 'shot' if they surface in the searchlight area (the underwater-swim section). The game may be played by beginners in shallow water, with a very short period of submergence. For advanced players, the degree of difficulty may be increased by:

- wearing clothes;
- carrying 'secret papers' (a kickboard);
- assisting an injured person;
- escaping with a personal injury, such as loss of the use of one limb;
- negotiating underwater 'hazards', such as a 'tunnel' (a series of anchored hoops);
- retrieving a satchel with escape directions in it.

FEET-FINDERS

Rationale   To introduce activities in which the players are unable to see.

Level   Beginner.

Equipment   Blackout goggles (one pair for each player), rubber bricks, weighted dive-rings, plastic bottles filled with water.

Depth of water   Waist-deep to shoulder-deep.

Number of participants   Whole class.

Organisation   Individual players.

Description   Players line up in the water, each with a pair of blackout goggles. Equipment is scattered on the bottom of the pool — at least one item per player. The area should be clearly defined: there should be lane ropes or buoyant ropes to prevent players from moving into deeper water or from one group to another. It should also be free of hazards.

On the word 'Go', the players put their goggles on and search with their feet for submerged objects. When one is found, the player retrieves it and returns to the starting point, all without removing the goggles. To assist players' return, the teacher may use voice, a tapping sound or music to give direction.

FLUTTER-RING DROP

Rationale   To develop confidence in underwater activities, including opening the eyes.

Level   Beginner.

Equipment   A set of flutter rings, obtainable from sports or swimming stores (each a different colour and showing a number, from one to six)

Depth of water   Waist-deep.

Number of participants   Groups of up to six.

Organisation   With individuals or small groups.

Description   The teacher 'throws' in the flutter rings, which slowly descend. If played individually, the child will attempt either to pick up the rings in number order or to retrieve them before they reach the bottom of the pool. If played with more than one child, the teacher can nominate the number or colour of the ring each must retrieve.

FOOT STOMPER

Rationale To encourage children to jump and move around in water.

Level Beginner.

Equipment None.

Depth of water Knee-deep to waist-deep.

Number of participants Up to whole class.

Organisation In pairs.

Description Pairs stand facing each other in the water, with hands on each other's shoulders. On the word 'Go', each tries to step on the other's feet, while at the same time avoiding being 'stomped on'.

FULL STOP

Rationale   To encourage effective sculling.

Level   Advanced.

Equipment   None.

Depth of water   Deep.

Number of participants   Up to whole class.

Organisation   Individual players.

Description   A player dives from the edge of the pool and immediately sculls with the hands, so that the feet remain above the water. The body remains in the inverted position.

GORDIAN KNOTS

This is a good water-safety game.

Rationale   To encourage opening the eyes underwater and holding the breath while performing a simple task.

Level   Beginner/intermediate.

Equipment   Metre lengths of nylon rope (one for each player).

Depth of water   Waist-deep.

Number of participants   Up to whole class.

Organisation   Individually and in pairs.

Description   Each person takes a length of rope, sits on the bottom of the pool (or leans forward with head and face submerged) and ties three simple knots in it. When working in pairs, players attempt (while underwater) to undo the knots they did not themselves tie.

Variations
1 Each person ties a length of rope around one leg, then tries to undo it while underwater.
2 Advanced swimmers can attempt to tie as many knots as possible for as long as they can remain underwater. When they surface, the knots are counted.

Note: This last activity requires **stringent** supervision.

HANDICAP TAG

Rationale   To develop and encourage a wide range of movements through water.

Level   Beginner/intermediate/advanced.

Equipment   None.

Depth of water   Ankle-deep to deep, according to level of skill.

Number of participants   Small groups up to whole class.

Organisation   Individual players.

Description   The teacher decides on the 'handicap' to be imposed — for example, hopping on the left leg with hands on head — while players try to get away from the person who is 'it'. All players must observe the handicap; any one who is tagged or who breaks the handicap conditions also becomes 'it'. The game continues until all players have been tagged or the teacher says 'Stop'.

Variation   For more advanced swimmers the handicap can be quite demanding; for example, using a butterfly action with one arm only.

HAZARD

Rationale   To acquaint players with strategies for coping with hazards in a natural environment.

Level   Advanced.

Equipment   Weighted hoops, blackout goggles, buoys, 'weeds' (plastic strips), buoyancy aids (assorted), small boat (vinyl) or polo bat, floating mat.

Depth of water   Deep.

Number of participants   Small groups to whole class.

Organisation   Groups working through a series of hazards or teams competing on identical courses.

Description   Teams or groups line up at one side of the pool and take turns to negotiate the hazards. A team member may not begin until the preceding one is out of the water. Tests include:
• negotiating weighted ropes at varying depths;
• swimming with blackout goggles around buoys;
• swimming through weed (long plastic strips attached to weighted, horizontal hoops);
• swimming through floating debris;
• swimming under an overturned boat (to air trapped beneath the boat) and out again;
• swimming under floating mats to simulate swimming under oil or petrol slicks.

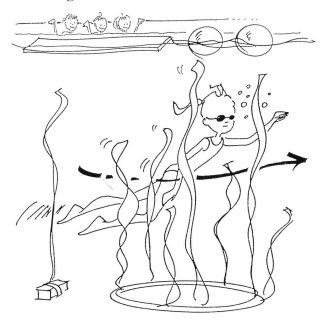

HOOP DIVE

Rationale   To teach treading water, surface diving and underwater swimming.

Level   Intermediate/advanced.

Equipment   Plastic or wooden hoops.

Depth of water   Deep.

Number of participants   Groups up to whole class.

Organisation   In groups of eight plus.

Description   Working in even groups (although that is not absolutely necessary), half the class form a circle holding hoops between them as shown in the illustration. The circle is thus 'complete'. The other half of the class tread water, each 'inside' a hoop but not holding it. When the teacher says 'One place change', each free swimmer does a feet-first dive to clear the hoop and then swims underwater to the next one to the right, surfacing within it. The teacher can call for a two- or three-place change according to the size of the class and the ability of the group.

HOOP-TOWING

Rationale   To develop advanced sculling techniques while towing a body that is in a good streamlined position.

Level   Advanced.

Equipment   Wooden hoops.

Depth of water   Waist-deep to deep.

Number of participants   Up to whole class.

Organisation   In pairs.

Description   Each pair of swimmers hook their feet under the rim of a hoop, lying opposite one another, as shown in the illustration. On the word 'Go', the one whose head is towards 'open' water sculls head first, towing the other feet first across or up the pool. When the pair reach the end, they reverse roles.

Variation   The person towing can *swim* backwards — backstroke or lifesaving backstroke — and this activity can be run between teams as a relay.

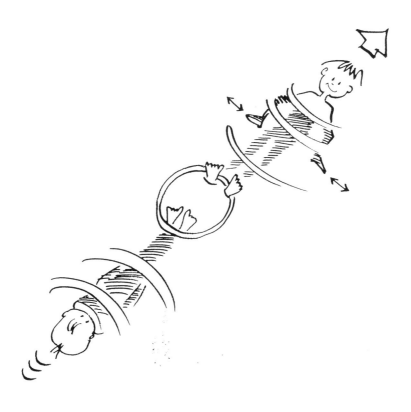

HOOP
UNDRESSING

This is a good water-safety activity.

Rationale   To encourage treading water and the removal of clothing below the surface.

Level   Intermediate/advanced.

Equipment   Hoops strung together, swimwear, long pants, long-sleeved shirts, shoes and socks.

Depth of water   Deep.

Number of participants   Up to whole class.

Organisation   Groups or teams of four to six.

Description   The hoops lie on the surface, strung across the pool. All players are dressed in swimwear, long pants, long-sleeved shirts, shoes and socks. On the word 'Go', the first member of each team dives or jumps into the water, swims to a hoop and ducks into the centre. Remaining inside the hoops, the swimmers have to remove their clothing and let it drop to the bottom of the pool, then surface-dive to retrieve it and swim with it to the side. It is then the turn of the next person in each team.

HOPPING CENTIPEDE

Rationale   To develop confidence in moving through water.

Level   Beginner.

Equipment   None.

Depth of water   Knee-deep to waist-deep.

Number of participants   Small groups.

Organisation   Teams of four to six.

Description   Teams stand in crocodile line facing across the pool, spaced about half a metre apart. Using both hands, each player holds the right leg of the one directly in front. On the word 'Go', the whole group hop from one side to the other. Once there, they change to hold left legs and hop back across the pool.

HOPPING COLLISIONS

Rationale   To encourage active movement in water and relaxation in case of a fall.

Level   Beginner.

Equipment   None.

Depth of water   Knee-deep to waist-deep.

Number of participants   Up to whole class.

Organisation   Individual players.

Description   Participants fold their arms and stand with one leg hooked behind the other. On the word 'Go', each one attempts to knock the nearest rival off balance by bumping and pushing (with arms still folded). If a player falls or touches the bottom with both feet, he or she is considered 'out'. The last one standing is the winner.

HORSES AND RIDERS

Rationale   To develop an understanding of buoyancy and how water can assist in weight-bearing.

Level   Beginner.

Equipment   None.

Depth of water   Waist-deep.

Number of participants   Up to whole class.

Organisation   In pairs.

Description   Paired players take turns to carry each other in piggyback fashion. On the word 'Go', the 'rider' scrambles right around the 'horse' three times, without touching the bottom of the pool or letting go, returning to the starting position. This can obviously be made into a race.

HUFF 'N PUFF

Rationale   To encourage strong exhalation.

Level   Beginner.

Equipment   Ping-pong balls, Saturn water toys (one for each player, or for each team).

Depth of water   Waist-deep.

Number of participants   Small groups to whole class.

Organisation   Individual players, each using a unit of equipment, or a team relay race.

Description   The players stand side by side at the starting point, each with a ping-pong ball. On the command 'Go' they enter the water and float the ball, then blow it along the surface of the water to the finish line. The ball may only be touched at the start and the finish.

Variations

1 If this activity is organised as a relay, no player may touch the ball at any time during the race.
2 The game may be made more challenging by including an obstacle course, with players blowing through hoops or around floats, or weaving between team members.

KICKBOARD TOSS

Rationale   To encourage accuracy when throwing a buoyant rescue aid.

Level   Beginner.

Equipment   A tethered hoop and three kickboards for each team.

Depth of water   Shallow.

Number of participants   Small groups to whole class.

Organisation   Teams of four working from edge to hoop and back; hoop 10 metres from edge (or at distance appropriate to ability of players).

Description   Members of each team line up on the edge of the pool opposite a hoop. The aim is to throw the kickboards so that they land within the hoop; each player uses all three kickboards and scores one point for each successful throw. When number 1 has thrown each board, that player enters the water, retrieves the boards and returns them to number 2, and so on until all team members have had a turn. The team with the highest score wins.

LONDON BRIDGE

Rationale   To develop water confidence, especially in submerging.

Level   Beginner.

Equipment   None.

Depth of water   Waist-deep.

Number of participants   Small groups to whole class.

Organisation   Groups of about six.

Description   Two members of each group join hands and form an arch; the rest walk under and around it. The arch is lowered slightly each time the end person passes through until eventually it rests on the surface, but the players still have to pass under the 'bridge'. The activity may be done to the accompaniment of players' singing 'London Bridge Is Falling Down'.

Remember to give the 'arch' a go!

MARCHING SOLDIER

Rationale   To encourage use of the correct streamlined position for the backstroke.

Level   Intermediate/advanced.

Equipment   None.

Depth of water   At least waist-deep.

Number of participants   Up to whole class.

Organisation   Individual players.

Description   Swimmers lie on their backs with left arms fully extended above the head and right arms fully extended on along the right leg. On the word 'Go' they perform flutter kicks across the pool while constantly reversing the position of the arms (right arm above the head, left arm on the left leg) but always keeping them out of the water. The action is similar to the normal backstroke, but the arms must never go under the water.

Note: If the position is not streamlined and the kick is not good enough, the body will sink!

MARK AND TAG

Rationale   To develop confidence in moving in a variety of ways through water.

Level   Beginner.

Equipment   None.

Depth of water   Ankle-deep to waist-deep.

Number of participants   Even numbers, up to whole class.

Organisation   In pairs.

Description   Paired swimmers stand one behind the other, facing in the same direction and about one arm's length apart; on the command 'Go', the one in front tries to 'get away' from the other. The teacher can stipulate the movement required — for instance, kangaroo jumping, hopping, skipping or running — which must be observed by both players. On the command 'Stop', both players stand and the one following should then still be within arm's distance of the one in front.

Variation   With more advanced groups, more difficult movement patterns can be used.

OP SHOP

This game may also be played at beginner and intermediate levels (see variation 1).

Rationale   To develop the techniques involved in swimming in clothing and to encourage speed in shedding wet clothing.

Level   Advanced.

Equipment   One pair of trousers, one shirt and one windcheater for each team. Clothes may be purchased inexpensively at an op shop.

Depth of water   Deep.

Number of participants   Small groups to whole class.

Organisation   Teams of four or more, across the pool.

Description   Each team lines up in shuttle relay formation (half the team on each side of the pool); the clothes are placed on the ground beside player number 1. On the command 'Go', number 1 dresses, dives into the pool, swims across to number 2, climbs out and undresses. Number 2 then repeats the sequence, as does each player until all have had a turn.

Variations
1   At beginner level this is played in waist-deep water; players use a slide-in entry and wade across the pool. At intermediate level, the water should be shoulder-deep, the entry as appropriate and the crossing made by either swimming or wading.
2   Various conditions may be placed on the players. For instance, a particular swimming stroke must be used, or propulsion must be by legs only, or by sculling.
3   Other articles of clothing, such as shoes, socks, hat or bag may be added.

OVER AND UNDER

Rationale   To encourage the freestyle flutter-kick action.

Level   Beginner/intermediate.

Equipment   Two 1 metre canes and two 1 metre hoops for each team.

Depth of water   Waist-deep.

Number of participants   Groups to whole class.

Organisation   Groups of ten or teams of ten or more.

Description   The players are numbered one to ten and are lined up in pairs about 1 metre apart, with 9 and 10 at the front and 1 and 2 at the back. Numbers 3 and 4, 7 and 8 hold the hoops and numbers 5 and 6, 9 and 10 hold the canes level between them. The hoops are held vertically, with the tops just above the surface; the canes are about 30–35 centimetres below the surface. Number 1 'torpedoes' through the hoops and over the canes without touching them, and number 2 follows. When both have passed over the last cane, they run outside the formation and change places with numbers 3 and 4, who repeat the sequence and change with 5 and 6. This procedure is repeated until numbers 9 and 10 have passed over the last cane; they then run a short distance to the finish line.

OVERHEAD BODY-PASSING

Rationale   To develop confidence in water, especially in bobbing below the surface.

Level   Beginner/intermediate.

Equipment   None.

Depth of water   Waist-deep.

Number of participants   Teams of about five.

Organisation   In crocodile line between start and finish, facing towards start.

Description   On the command 'Go', the team leader lies on his or her back in the water. The others duck under the water in turn and pass the 'body' over their heads along the line. When the leader reaches the end of the line and resumes a standing position, the next one in front becomes the 'body'. This continues until everyone has had a turn.

PAIRED SWIMMING

Rationale   To demonstrate that arms and legs are both important in a stroke. It may also be used to provide *active resistance* for the competent swimmer and to help with streamlining.

Level   Advanced.

Equipment   None.

Depth of water   Waist-deep.

Number of participants   Even numbers up to whole class.

Organisation   In pairs.

Description   Both swimmers adopt the prone position for freestyle, one behind the other; the rear person holds the ankles of the one in front, who provides the arm propulsion. The one at the back provides the leg propulsion. They work in unison to propel themselves from one side of the pool to the other, and then change places.

Variation   This obviously can be done on the back, with the first swimmer's legs hooked under the armpits of the second. Other strokes also can be attempted. Be adventurous!

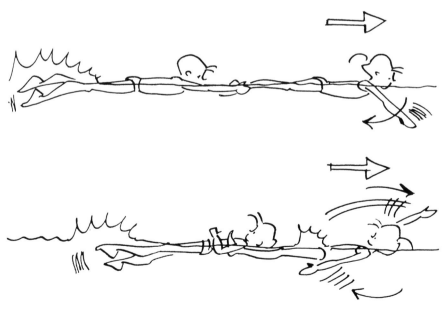

THE PENCIL
AND THE PEA

Rationale   To develop streamlining and to encourage good flutter-kicking techniques.

Level   Intermediate/advanced.

Equipment   Water-polo balls or equivalent.

Depth of water   Waist-deep to deep.

Number of participants   Small groups.

Organisation   Teams of six to eight.

Description   Groups are divided in half and are placed on either side of the pool, the halves facing each other in crocodile lines. The aim is for players to push the ball across the pool using the head only, while performing a flutter kick. Their arms may be at their sides or on either side of the ball, but below the surface. Number 1 in each team pushes the ball first; number 2 returns with it across the pool. This continues until everyone has had a turn.

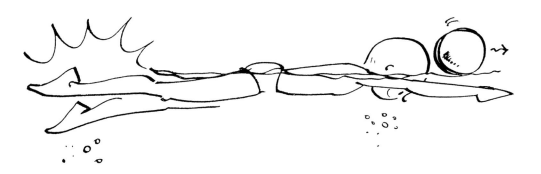

PFD EXCHANGE RELAY

Rationale To develop the skill of putting on and removing a PFD in deep water.

Level Intermediate/advanced.

Equipment PFDs suitable for the age group.

Depth of water Deep.

Number of participants Small groups to whole class.

Organisation Groups of about four.

Description Half of each group should be standing on either side of the pool with a PFD floating between them in the middle. On the word 'Go', the first player dives, swims to the PFD, puts it on *fully*, takes it off (leaving it in the same spot) and swims across to the second player, who then does the same. The game continues until all group members have completed this sequence.

Variation This can be done as a relay or as a timed event.

PINBALL

Rationale   To develop the skills and techniques involved in sculling.

Level   Intermediate/advanced.

Equipment   20 centimetre ball or equivalent.

Depth of water   Waist-deep.

Number of participants   Even number, up to whole class.

Organisation   In pairs.

Description   Players lie in a supine position with their feet towards each other. The ball is placed in such a position that together they can hold it between the soles of their feet. They then scull — one going feet first and the other head first — to the other side of the pool (or another predetermined mark), keeping the ball all the time in the same position. This can be done as a race or a relay, with pairs competing against each other to get 'there and back' first.

PIRATE PETE

Rationale   To encourage confident entry, exit and movement through water.

Level   Beginner.

Equipment   None.

Depth of water   Shallow.

Number of participants   Small groups to whole class.

Organisation   Across the whole pool.

Description   Players stand at one side of the pool. Pirate Pete is in the water, a little distance from the edge, walking to and fro and asking: 'Who's afraid of Pirate Pete?'. Players answer: 'Not I'. When Pirate Pete answers 'Yes, you are!', all players must enter the water and try to reach the opposite side without being caught by Pete. Those caught become pirates and help Pirate Pete to catch the rest. The winner is the last player caught, who then becomes Pirate Pete in the next game.

RAFTING

Rationale   To encourage swimmers to tread water.

Level   Intermediate/advanced.

Equipment   Ropes, plastic fruit-juice or detergent containers with handles and lids, car-tyre inner tubes, smooth wooden planks of manageable size (selection of articles distributed to each team).

Depth of water   Deep.

Number of participants   Small groups to whole class.

Organisation   Teams raft-building and a race.

Description   Each team's equipment is at the edge of the pool. All team members are in the water except one, who remains on the edge to issue equipment as needed. Players work together to build a raft; they must use all the pieces of equipment, and no player in the water may touch the edge of the pool. When all equipment has been issued, the last player joins the team in the water. The completed raft is paddled to the other end of the pool, all team members holding on to it. The raft must be intact at the finish.

RESCUE-TUBE RELAY

Rationale   To develop the techniques involved in the use of the rescue tube.

Level   Advanced.

Equipment   One rescue tube for each team.

Depth of water   Minimum of shoulder depth.

Number of participants   Small groups to whole class.

Organisation   One small group or teams of up to eight with larger groups.

Description   Each team lines up with the leader (number 1) at one end or side of the pool and the other players at the other. The rescue tube is placed on the ground in front of the leader. On the command 'Go', number 1 dons the rescue-tube band, dives in and swims to number 2, who is waiting in the water. Number 1 passes the tube to number 2, who holds it across the chest and under the arms; number 1 then swims behind 2, fastens the tube and swims back to the starting point, where they both climb out. Number 2 takes off the tube, with assistance from number 1, then repeats the process with number 3. The sequence continues until all players are at the starting point.

RIDING THE RAPIDS

Rationale   To assist players to move through the water.

Level   Beginner.

Equipment   None.

Depth of water   Shallow.

Number of participants   Groups of ten or twelve to whole class.

Organisation   Players in two lines, 1.5 metres apart and facing each other, so forming a 'tube'.

Description   The two players at the starting end push off and glide into the tube. The standing players rhythmically sweep the water in the direction of travel, all using both hands, and the floating players are moved along the 'rapids'. When they reach the end they join the standing players and the next two begin. This continues until all have had a turn.

ROLL-OVER BALL

Rationale To teach the techniques of sculling and body rotation.

Level Advanced.

Equipment A soccer-size ball for each group or team.

Depth of water Waist-deep.

Number of participants Small groups to whole class.

Organisation Single file with a small group or teams of five or six with larger groups.

Description Players stand in the pool, about 1 metre apart, in a single crocodile line. The team leader holds the ball. On the command 'Go', all players lie on their backs and commence a 'holding' scull. The leader places the ball between his or her feet and attempts to pass it over the head to the second player, who in turn will use his or her feet to take the ball and pass it on in the same way while all maintain their sculling action. This continues down the line until the ball reaches the last player, who can then hold it while running or swimming to the front of the line. This continues until the leader is once again at the front.

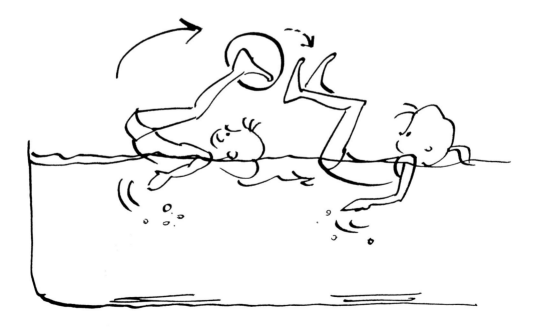

ROPE-THROWING RELAY

Rationale To practise the rope-throwing rescue technique in a fun way.

Level Intermediate/advanced.

Equipment 10 metre lengths of nylon throwing ropes.

Depth of water Chest-deep to deep.

Number of participants Small groups to whole class.

Organisation Groups of four to six.

Description The group leader stands out of the water with a 10 metre throwing rope lying uncoiled by his or her feet. The rest of the team, in the pool, stand or tread water one behind the other, the first one about 9 metres from the edge. On the word 'Go', the leader coils the rope, throws it to the first person in line and pulls that person to the side. This player then gets out of the pool and 'rescues' the next in line. This continues until all the team are 'safe'. This can be run as a relay race.

Variation The first person may stand in the line, swim to the side and get out of the water before throwing the rope.

ROTISSERIE

Rationale   To encourage the technique of flutter kick, and rotation of the body.

Level   Intermediate.

Equipment   None.

Depth of water   Chest-deep.

Number of participants   Small group to whole class.

Organisation   As a race for individuals or as a relay.

Description   Players perform a designated number of kicks (for instance, four or eight) in four positions — face down, on the left side, on the back and on the right side — while effecting a complete roll-over. Arms are held by the sides.

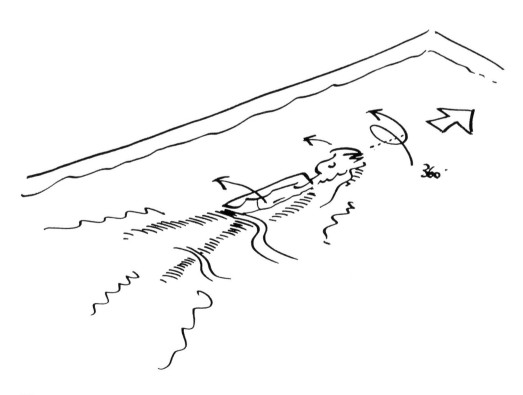

SCARECROW CIRCLE

Rationale To develop confidence

Level Beginner.

Equipment None.

Depth of water Waist-deep.

Number of participants Small groups to whole class.

Organisation In pairs.

Description One partner stands with feet apart, arms stretched out sideways and just touching the surface of the water. The other stands behind. On the word 'Go', the one behind has to run around the other, ducking under the water to pass below the arms. This is usually done about three times, after which the runner crawls or swims between the other's legs to take up the front position and adopt the 'scarecrow stance'. The second player now becomes the runner.

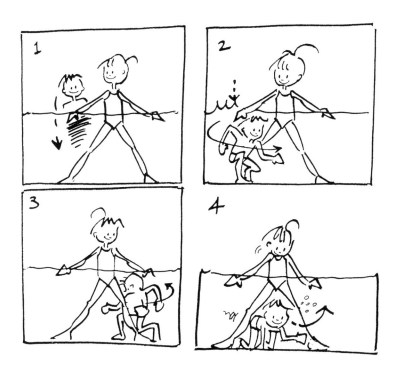

SIAMESE TWINS

Rationale   To develop the techniques of contact rescue.

Level   Advanced.

Equipment   None.

Depth of water   Shoulder-deep minimum.

Number of participants   Small groups to whole class.

Organisation   Small groups in pairs, large groups in teams of four, six or eight.

Description   Players working in pairs start and finish at the same point. Number 1 grasps number 2 in the designated contact-rescue grip and tows to a rope, buoy or any predetermined mark, where the two change places. Number 2 then tows number 1 back to the starting point. This is repeated by the second pair, and so on until each pair has had a turn.

Variation   This format may also be used with aided rescues.

SKILLS RACE

Rationale To develop the techniques of a variety of skills.

Level Intermediate/advanced.

Equipment None.

Depth of water 1.8 metre minimum.

Number of participants Small groups to whole class.

Organisation Individual swimming, across the pool.

Description Players stand at the edge of the pool, and are told the specific skill to be used. On the command 'Go', they dive into the water and begin to swim towards the finish. On a signal from the teacher, all perform the designated skill, then continue swimming to the final line. The skill signal may be given as often as is practicable. Suitable skills may include:
- treading water for a given time;
- stationary sculling;
- surface dives, both head first and feet first;
- somersaults, forward and back;
- vertical rotation, using legs only;
- floating — a designated float.

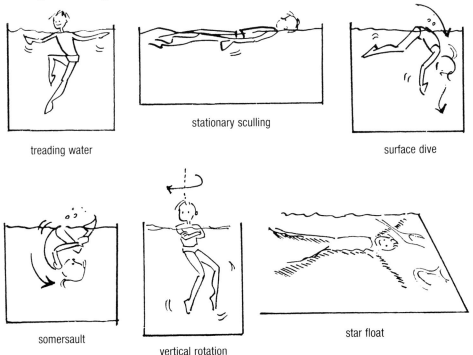

treading water

stationary sculling

surface dive

somersault

vertical rotation

star float

SURF RESCUE

Rationale To experience contact rescue in simulated rough water.

Level Advanced.

Equipment None.

Depth of water Waist-deep to shoulder-deep.

Number of participants Small groups to whole class.

Organisation Groups of eight, teams of eight to twelve or whole class.

Description Players stand in the water facing the edge of the pool, holding the rail. To create the waves, they first push vigorously away from the wall and then push towards it, and this action is sustained as the first two players perform a contact tow behind the line. When these two have reached the end of the turbulent water, players 3 and 4 begin a contact tow and those on the wall move down two places, while players 1 and 2 join the end of the line. This is repeated until all pairs have had a turn.

To make this a race, two groups of even numbers work on either side of the pool in water of similar depth.

Option To create turbulence, small boats (such as canoe polo bats) may be used. They are placed at the side of the pool and players sit on the edge with their feet in the boats and rock them from side to side.

THERE AND BACK

Rationale   To develop techniques of contact rescue.

Level   Advanced.

Equipment   None.

Depth of water   Shallow to deep.

Number of participants   At least four.

Organisation   Small group or teams, preferably with eight in a team.

Description   In a team of eight, seven players line up at one end of the pool and number 1 stands at the other end. On 'Go', number 1 dives in, swims to number 2, grasps that player in the designated contact tow and swims to the starting point. Number 2 then returns for number 3, and so on until everyone has been towed to the starting point.

THREAD THE NEEDLE

Rationale   To encourage confidence in entering water and in submerging.

Level   Beginner.

Equipment   Ropes and plastic hoops.

Depth of water   Waist-deep.

Number of participants   Small groups to whole class.

Organisation   Six floating hoops tethered to the side of the pool at a distance of no more than 30 centimetres and about 1 metre apart.

Description   Players line up at the first hoop. Player 1 jumps into hoop 1, submerges, resurfaces in hoop 2, climbs out of the pool and then repeats the sequence with hoops 3 and 4, and hoops 5 and 6. When player 1 finishes, player 2 starts and completes the sequence. This continues until all have been through it once.

Variations
1 To make this a race, have two sets of hoops tethered at either side of the pool at the same depth, or along the shallow-end wall.
2 During submersion, players pick objects off the pool bottom from beneath hoops 2, 4 and 6.

TIED UP

This is a water-safety activity.

Rationale To encourage swimmers to keep calm and use their buoyancy to advantage if they become caught in ropes, rigging or other entanglements.

Level Advanced.

Equipment Lifesaving throwing ropes of 10 metre lengths.

Depth of water Deep.

Number of participants Up to whole class.

Organisation *Always at least* in pairs.

Description One of each pair *loosely* wraps a length of throwing rope around the body of the other from head to foot. *No knots are used.* The first swimmer then enters the water, standing facing the pool side and a short distance from it. The tied swimmer jumps into the water between the partner and the wall and immediately begins to unravel the rope. When this is done, the second person has a turn.

Note: In most cases, much of the rope comes away from the body as it enters the water, leaving very little to be released. *However, the 'free' swimmer must be in the water before the tied swimmer jumps in. This is simply a safety precaution, so that should the tied swimmer have any difficulty at all he or she can at once be pinned to the wall by the partner.*

TOE DROP-OFF RELAY

Rationale   To develop confidence and teach streamlining.

Level   Beginner/intermediate.

Equipment   None.

Depth of water   Waist-deep.

Number of participants   Even numbers up to whole class.

Organisation   Teams of about five across the width of the pool.

Description   Player number 1 faces across the pool to the rest of the team, who are standing one behind the other on the other side. On the word 'Go', number 1 runs (or swims) across the pool, catches the left big toe of number 2 and (walking, not swimming) tows that player back across the pool. When number 2's feet touch the wall, he or she stands up and goes back for number 3. This continues until all members of the team have been towed across the pool to the starting point.

TOPSY-TURVY

Rationale To develop advanced sculling techniques and water skills.

Level Advanced.

Equipment None.

Depth of water Deep.

Number of participants Up to whole class.

Organisation Individual players.

Description Spaced at safe distances, swimmers scull in the vertical position. The teacher calls out different tasks to be performed, such as:
- feet-first dive, touch the bottom and surface;
- rotate vertically to right or left;
- do a forward or backward roll;
- float on front or back;
- tread water with:
  - fingers out
  - wrists out
  - elbows just touching the water
  - arms in the air

Just for fun, the final task is to scull upside down in a handstand position, with the lower legs together and clear of the water.

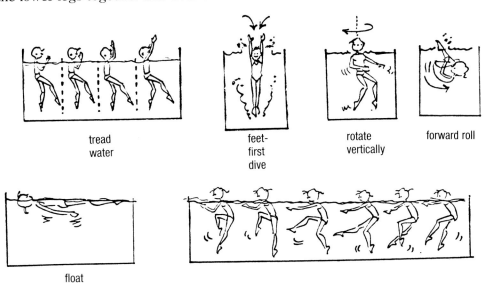

tread
water

feet-
first
dive

rotate
vertically

forward roll

float

TORPEDO TUBE

Rationale   To teach the principles involved in streamlining.

Level   Beginner.

Equipment   None.

Depth of water   Waist-deep.

Number of participants   Small groups to whole class.

Organisation   Teams of four or five, standing sideways on and almost shoulder to shoulder across the working area.

Description   On the command 'Go', player 1 lies face down and still in the water, with arms extended beyond the head. The others will pull this player by the arms along the 'torpedo tube' to the end of the line. Player 1 then stands up and joins the line, and player 2 becomes the 'torpedo'. This continues until all players have had a turn.

Variation   This can also be done on the back, with arms extended beyond the head, as well as in a 'tight-ball' shape. This latter position creates massive resistance to the body and makes it difficult to move. Try different body positions. Children quickly work out that 'long and thin' is the best shape!

TRASH AND
TREASURE

Rationale   To encourage confidence in submerging and in opening eyes underwater.

Level   Beginner.

Equipment   For each player: 1 small buoyant object (plastic-bottle cap), 1 cork, 1 numbered flutter disc, 1 weighted diving ring, 1 ping-pong ball, 1 two cent coin, 1 small plastic container.

Depth of water   Shallow.

Number of participants   Small groups to whole class.

Organisation   Individual players.

Description   Players line up at the edge of the pool, each with a plastic container. All equipment is scattered on the water. On the command 'Go', players enter the water and collect one complete set of equipment. The first to do this is the winner.

TUMBLEWEEDS

This is a good water-safety activity.

Rationale   To develop the basic skills involved in learning a tumble-turn.

Level   Intermediate.

Equipment   None.

Depth of water   1 metre plus.

Number of participants   Up to whole class.

Organisation   Beginning individually, later in pairs.

Description   Swimmers stand about 6 metres from the side wall and well spaced. On the word 'Go' they swim or flutter kick to the wall, touch it with both hands and perform a forward roll. Without touching bottom, they push off with both feet and flutter kick on their backs to the starting point. All complete this sequence.

Variation   When working in pairs, the second swimmer is a couple of seconds behind the first. When the first one rolls off the wall, he or she remains underwater and swims below the second swimmer, watching the latter pass over.

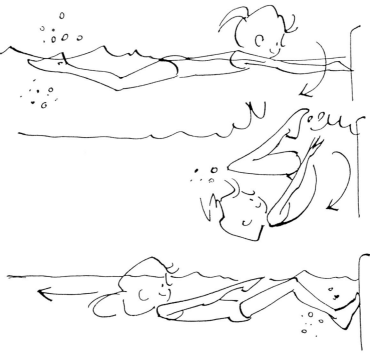

TUNNEL BRICK

Rationale To develop confidence and underwater swimming.

Level Beginner/intermediate.

Equipment Rubber bricks.

Depth of water Waist-deep.

Number of participants Teams of about five.

Organisation Players one behind the other in crocodile line.

Description In this game each player must have his or her head underwater, with eyes open, to receive a rubber brick from the player in front and pass it to the one behind. Team members stand one behind the other and about half a metre apart. The leader holds a rubber brick. On the word 'Go', the leader bends and passes the brick through his or her legs into the hands of the player behind. When the brick reaches the end of the line, the last person will swim with it through the legs of all the players to the front of the line, where the process is repeated until every player has had a turn.

It is quite permissible for the underwater swimmer to surface between players in order to take a breath!

TWO BY TWO

Rationale To encourage concentration on the propulsive action of strokes.

Level Intermediate/advanced.

Equipment None.

Depth of water Chest-deep to deep.

Number of participants Small groups to whole class.

Organisation In pairs, across width or length of pool.

Description Players line up in pairs, holding inside hands.
Swimming together, they perform the following actions:
- butterfly, using a dolphin kick and outside arms only;
- freestyle, using outside arms and flutter kick;
- backstroke, using outside arms and flutter kick;
- breaststroke, using outside arms and whip kick;
- lifesaving backstroke, using outside arms and inverted whip kick.

For sidestroke ('Teaspoons'), players face the same way and swim in unison.
The one behind holds the other at the waist.

WALL OF DEATH

Rationale   To practise techniques used in escaping from an unexpected grasp.

Level   Advanced.

Equipment   None.

Depth of water   Deep.

Number of participants   Up to whole class.

Organisation   In groups of eight to ten, along the side of the pool.

Description   Players form a line in the water, holding the wall. Among them is the 'attacker'. One starts at the deep end and slowly swims past the line, eyes closed. Those left in line splash and talk, to cover the movement of the attacker. The teacher designates the attacker to grab the swimmer from either the front or the back, and in one of the following ways:
• around the neck
• around the waist
• around the hips
• around the legs
Each player takes a turn at being swimmer or attacker until everyone has played each role.

Safety point: The swimmer should stop struggling if he or she feels unable to get free in a reasonable time, and both swimmer and attacker surface immediately.

WATERY CHATS

Rationale To develop confidence in sitting on the bottom of the pool and opening the eyes underwater.

Level Beginner/intermediate.

Equipment None.

Depth of water Waist-deep.

Number of participants Up to whole class.

Organisation In pairs.

Description Pairs sit on the bottom of the pool and shake hands, meanwhile having a short 'conversation' — for example, they tell each other their names, their ages and where they live. With older groups the teacher can decide on a topic, such as the weather! The game finishes when the pairs return to a standing position.

WEED WALL

Rationale   To develop the technique of moving through weeds or kelp.

Level   Beginner.

Equipment   Strips of plastic attached to weighted hoops (use plastic garbage bags).

Depth of water   Shallow.

Number of participants   Small groups to whole class.

Organisation   Teams of four to six.

Description   Teams line up at the edge of the pool in crocodile line with the 'wall of weeds' in place along the middle of the playing area. Players in turn enter the water, wade across the pool through the weeds, touch the other side and wade back through the weeds to the starting point. The first team to finish is the winner.

'WHAT'S THE TIME, MR WOLF?'

This is a very old primary school game, adapted for the water.

Rationale   To develop confidence in water through active movement.

Level   Beginner.

Equipment   None.

Depth of water   Knee-deep to waist-deep.

Number of participants   Small groups.

Organisation   Groups of about six.

Description   One member of the group is designated the wolf and stands facing away from the rest, who are standing near the pool wall. The wolf walks away, followed by the other players, who chant 'What's the time Mr Wolf?'. The wolf usually says '1 o'clock', '3 o'clock' or '7 o'clock' and so on and keeps walking, while the others keep following. If the wolf says 'Dinner time!', he or she turns and chases the group back to the wall, attempting to tag as many of them as possible. The last person to be tagged is the winner.

Variation   Both wolf and followers may swim when the hunt is on!

WHIRLPOOL

Rationale   To experience the feel of a current.

Level   Beginner.

Equipment   None.

Depth of water   Waist-deep.

Number of participants   Whole class.

Organisation   A circle with players spaced at arm's length.

Description   When players start running while keeping circle formation, they create a current. When this — the whirlpool — is formed they may stop running and float, and so experience being carried along by moving water. Floating should be on front, back and side. At a signal from the teacher, players all change direction and try running or swimming against the current.

WRITHING
SNAKE

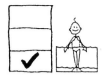

Rationale   To develop confidence in water through active movement.

Level   Beginner.

Equipment   None.

Depth of water   Ankle-deep to waist-deep.

Number of participants   Small groups to whole class.

Organisation   Groups of three or four, with players numbered.

Description   In each group, number 1 player faces the others, who are standing one behind the other and each holding the waist of the person in front. On the command 'Go', number 1 tries to tag the last in the line, who is 'protected' by the other members of the team; they do this by constantly moving (writhing) (without letting go of each other) and getting in the way of number 1. When the end person is tagged, he or she becomes the catcher, number 1 moves to the head of the snake and the game begins again.

'AHOY THERE!'

RESCUE-SKILLS CIRCUIT

Rationale   To practise reach, throw and wade rescues.

Level   Beginner.

Equipment   Kickboards, unweighted ropes, weighted ropes, balls, car-tyre inner tubes, esky lids, PFDs, assorted buoyant aids, rigid aids, towels, clothing.

Depth of water   Shallow.

Number of participants   Small groups to whole class.

Organisation   In pairs, moving from station to station in numbered order.

Description   This circuit requires use of a shallow pool.

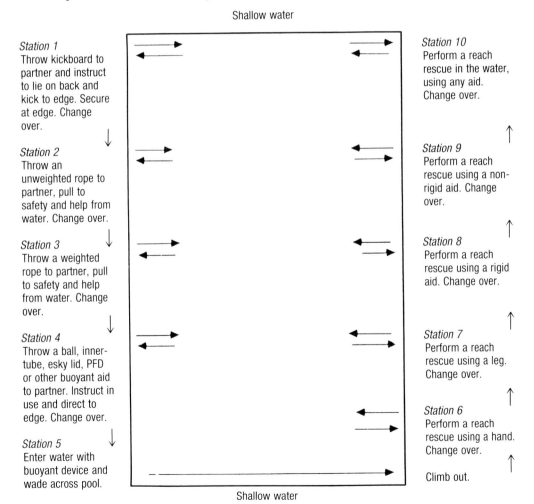

Shallow water

Station 1
Throw kickboard to partner and instruct to lie on back and kick to edge. Secure at edge. Change over.

Station 2
Throw an unweighted rope to partner, pull to safety and help from water. Change over.

Station 3
Throw a weighted rope to partner, pull to safety and help from water. Change over.

Station 4
Throw a ball, inner-tube, esky lid, PFD or other buoyant aid to partner. Instruct in use and direct to edge. Change over.

Station 5
Enter water with buoyant device and wade across pool.

Station 10
Perform a reach rescue in the water, using any aid. Change over.

Station 9
Perform a reach rescue using a non-rigid aid. Change over.

Station 8
Perform a reach rescue using a rigid aid. Change over.

Station 7
Perform a reach rescue using a leg. Change over.

Station 6
Perform a reach rescue using a hand. Change over.

Climb out.

Shallow water

AID AND ABET

RESCUE-SKILLS CIRCUIT

Rationale   To practise in-water, non-contact rescues.

Level   Intermediate.

Equipment   Buoyant aids, non-buoyant aids, boogie board, surf mat, surfboard.

Depth of water   Chest-deep to deep.

Number of participants   Small groups to whole class.

Organisation   In pairs, moving from station to station in numbered order.

Description

Station 1
Enter water, using compact jump.

Station 3
Secure partner at edge of pool.
Instruct to climb out.

Station 4
Using a boogie board, surf mat or
surf board, paddle across pool to
partner. Take partner on board and
return.

Station 5
Using a buoyant aid, perform a
non-contact tow.

Station 6
Using a non-buoyant aid, perform a
non-contact tow.

Station 7
Using a stirrup lift, land partner.

Station 8
In groups of eight, perform the
human-chain rescue.

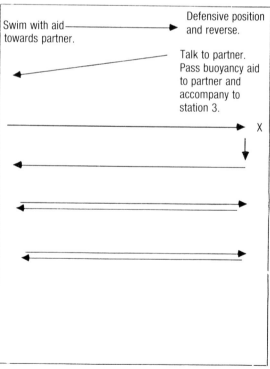

Deep water

Swim with aid towards partner.

Defensive position and reverse.

Station 2

Talk to partner.
Pass buoyancy aid
to partner and
accompany to
station 3.

X

Shallow water

'GOT YOU!'

RESCUE-SKILLS CIRCUIT

Rationale   To practise contact rescue.

Level   Advanced.

Equipment   Buoyant aids of varying sizes, spinal board.

Depth of water   Shallow to deep.

Number of participants   Small groups to whole class.

Organisation   In pairs, moving from station to station in numbered order.

Description   Circuit is to be completed with participants dressed in shirts and trousers.

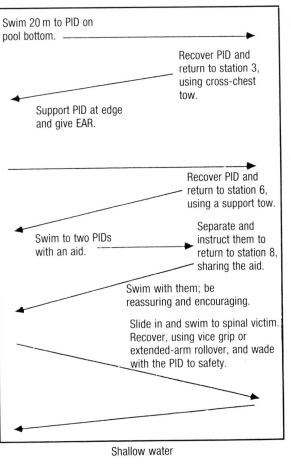

Deep water

Station 1
Enter using the slide, from a low height, e.g. starting blocks.

Station 3
Land PID, using straight-arm lift. Check for vital signs.

Station 4
Using a buoyant aid, swim to PID.

Station 6
Support PID at edge and land now-conscious person, using stirrup lift.

Station 8
Use drag method to move one PID to shallow water. Instruct the other to climb out.

Station 10
Enlist help of bystanders. Using spinal board, land PID.

Swim 20 m to PID on pool bottom.

Recover PID and return to station 3, using cross-chest tow.

Support PID at edge and give EAR.

Recover PID and return to station 6, using a support tow.

Separate and instruct them to return to station 8, sharing the aid.

Swim to two PIDs with an aid.

Swim with them; be reassuring and encouraging.

Slide in and swim to spinal victim. Recover, using vice grip or extended-arm rollover, and wade with the PID to safety.

Station 2
Depth 2 m. No spinal injury; no aids are available.

Station 5
Small buoyant aids only are available.

Station 7
Use medium-size buoyant aid — car-tyre inner tube.

Station 9
While waiting, perform EAR. Clear water. Call for help.

Shallow water

'MADE IT!'
SURVIVAL CIRCUIT

Rationale   To encourage the practice of survival skills.

Level   Beginner.

Equipment   One kickboard for each player, three weighted hoops, two buckets, small stones (one per player), weighted buoy.

Depth of water   Shallow.

Number of participants   Small groups to whole class.

Organisation   Individual, moving from station to station in numbered order.

Description

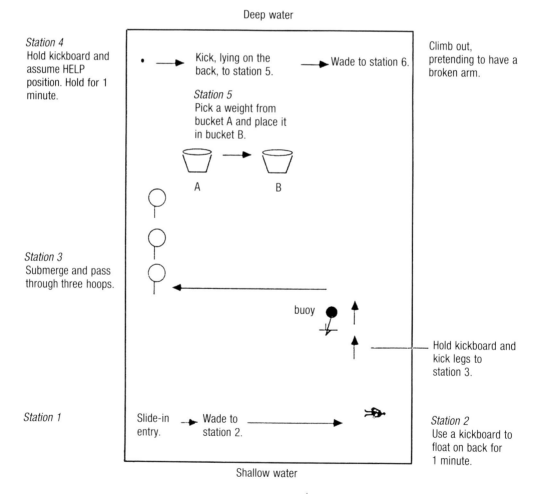

Deep water

Station 4
Hold kickboard and assume HELP position. Hold for 1 minute.

Kick, lying on the back, to station 5.

Wade to station 6.

Climb out, pretending to have a broken arm.

Station 5
Pick a weight from bucket A and place it in bucket B.

A   B

Station 3
Submerge and pass through three hoops.

buoy

Hold kickboard and kick legs to station 3.

Station 1

Slide-in entry.

Wade to station 2.

Station 2
Use a kickboard to float on back for 1 minute.

Shallow water

STAY ALIVE

SURVIVAL CIRCUIT

Rationale   To develop survival skills.

Level   Intermediate.

Equipment   Two tethered hoops, PFDs.

Depth of water   Chest-deep to deep.

Number of participants   Small groups to whole class.

Organisation   Individual, moving from station to station in numbered order.

Description

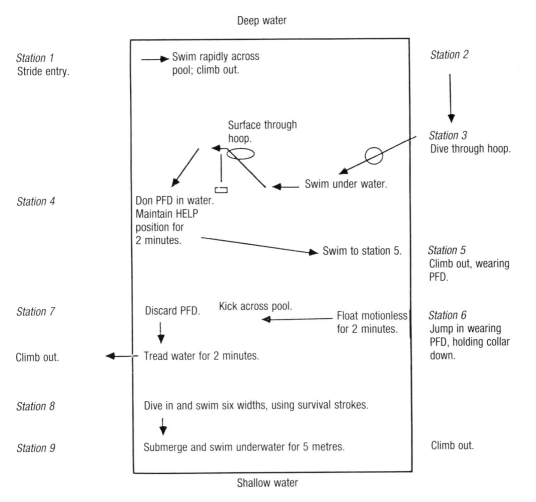

Deep water

Station 1
Stride entry.

Swim rapidly across pool; climb out.

Station 2

Surface through hoop.

Station 3
Dive through hoop.

Swim under water.

Station 4
Don PFD in water. Maintain HELP position for 2 minutes.

Swim to station 5.

Station 5
Climb out, wearing PFD.

Station 7
Discard PFD.

Kick across pool.

Float motionless for 2 minutes.

Station 6
Jump in wearing PFD, holding collar down.

Climb out.

Tread water for 2 minutes.

Station 8
Dive in and swim six widths, using survival strokes.

Station 9
Submerge and swim underwater for 5 metres.

Climb out.

Shallow water

SURVIVE

SURVIVAL CIRCUIT

Rationale   To develop endurance and to practise survival skills.

Level   Advanced.

Equipment   Trousers, shirt and jumper for each participant, tethered hoops, weighted hoops, rubber bricks, blackout goggles, assorted buoyancy devices.

Depth of water   Deep.

Number of participants   Small groups to whole class.

Organisation   Individual, moving from station to station in numbered order.

Description

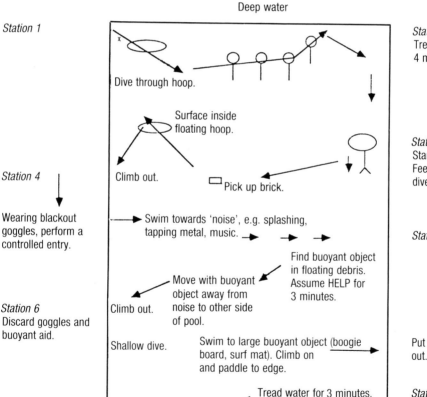